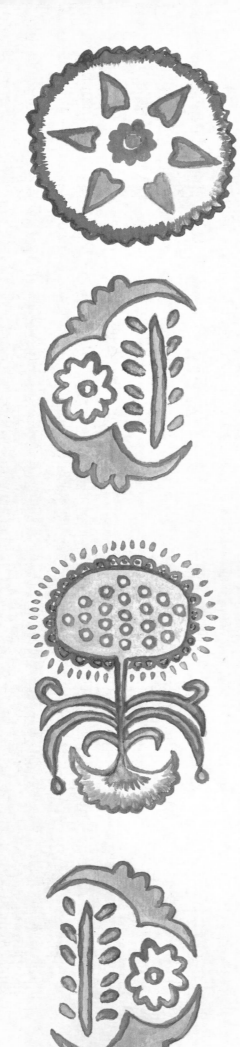

For my dear mother, Elena, with eternal gratitude for her love and care, for her example of inexhaustible creativity, for her support of my many ideas, and for not getting angry at me when she found me bathing in her freshly-made apricot syrup.

Marina Abrams

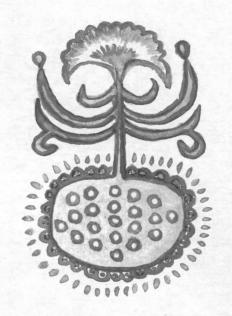

Orange and Blue:
The World of Barzu

*Stories about a boy named Barzu,
his family, and the world of wonders
and legends that surrounds him.*

Book One

Translated from the Russian by Joshua Abrams

Illustrations by Farrukh Negmatzade
and Marina Abrams

Barzu World 2018

On the Road to Grandmother's House

Far, far past the horizon there is a marvelous land of deserts and steppe, of swift rivers flowing past age-old cities, and of blue lakes glistening beneath towering mountains. This is the ancient land of Central Asia!

And in a southern corner of that vast region people built their homes right on the high mountain slopes and planted gardens where, in summer, the most delicious fruits ripen - apricots, grapes, and the sweetest melons.

In one such village – or *kishlak* – lives a curious and playful boy named Barzu. Every day he rides about on his bicycle to meet his friends, or go to his father's workshop, or visit his grandmother in the next kishlak. Running along after him is his faithful dog, Azhdar, and Barzu is always sure to bring his *nai*, a small flute he loves to play. Whoever he meets he tries to help and so everyone around knows him as the kindest of boys.

More than anything, Barzu loves to eat the freshly baked bread his grandmother makes, which in Central Asia is called *nan* or *non*. And even more than that, Barzu loves to watch her bake it in the *tanoor*, a round clay oven with a wide opening at the top.

Early in the morning, Barzu's grandmother prepares the dough, then she lights a fire in the tanoor and waits for the wood to burn down to glowing red embers. She adds small branches from fruit trees to the fire for a special aroma and taste. While the wood is burning down, Barzu's grandmother separates and kneads the dough into balls and then presses them down into round, flat shapes.

She decorates each non with pretty designs made by a small stamping tool called a *nonpar*. The nonpar is made out of the wood of a fruit tree with thin metal nails. Craftsmen hammer the nails into a variety of patterns such as the sun or stars, petals, flowers, and even birds. Grandmother bought ten nonpars at the bazaar so she can give her non different designs each time she bakes.

7

Before putting the dough in the tanoor, Grandmother rubs one side with milk and sesame seeds. This will make the baked non turn a beautiful red-gold, like the sun. She sprinkles the other side with water so that the bread will adhere to the walls of the tanoor without sticking. Donning a long, thick mitten that goes up to her elbow, Grandmother presses each non onto the inside walls of the tanoor. Just for Barzu, she will usually bake a few smaller non, as well, called *kulcha*.

After a little while, the bread is ready and Grandmother takes them out of the tanoor with a long-handled spatula and ladle. She uses the spatula to scrape each non off the oven wall, catches it in the ladle, and then drops the hot bread onto the table. Barzu stands nearby, waiting impatiently for his bread. As soon as he can, he grabs a piping hot kulcha from the table, tosses it from hand to hand and blows on it, to keep from burning his fingers. Joyfully, Barzu eats the aromatic, chewy bread and always declares to his grandmother, "This is the best bread in the world!"

However, Grandmother's tanoor was already quite old and Barzu's father decided to make her a new one. After all, his father is none other than Master Zafar, the best tanoor-maker in the mountains. Everyone around buys his tanoors!

11

And so, early one morning Barzu was wakened by Ravshan, his older brother, saying, "Get up, little brother! Grandmother's new tanoor is ready, and we have to bring it to her. Let's go together!"

Barzu dressed quickly, ate his breakfast, and went out to help hitch the tanoor to Ravshan's bicycle. It was a sunny, summer day. Ravshan slowly towed the heavy tanoor, while Barzu pedaled light and free on his own bike. Everything around them brought joy: the dear and familiar mountains holding up the deep blue sky, birds singing, the blooming mountain grasses filling the air with sweet fragrances. Azhdar frolicked happily ahead of the boys.

Suddenly, Barzu saw two girls he knew, Sitora and Lola. They were climbing down to the mountain river to fill their buckets with water. The girls were arguing together loudly.

"You keep going, Ravshan," he called to his brother, "I'll catch up later!" He biked down to the girls and greeted them.

"Oh! Barzu! Are you headed to your grandmother's?" asked Lola.

"Yes, my brother and I are bringing her a new tanoor so she can bake more delicious non for us. What are you arguing about so loudly?"

"You see, our father gave us two necklaces for a present. One has coral beads and the other has turquoise, and he told us that we should decide ourselves who will keep which. It has already been a week and we still can't decide. We each like both the coral and the turquoise beads," answered Sitora.

Barzu laughed – this was such a simple problem to fix! "Give me your necklaces and a handkerchief!" he said. As soon as they handed them over to him, he sat on the ground and pulled the beads off of each necklace, onto the cloth.

The girls cried out, "Why did you pull them apart?! What will we tell our father? Now neither of us has a necklace!"

But Barzu went straight to work, threading the beads back onto each piece of string – first one coral bead, then a turquoise, then another coral bead, then another turquoise. When he was done, he gave each sister a necklace with the beads mixed together.

Lola and Sitora were so happy, they clapped their hands, put on their necklaces, and began to sing and dance! Barzu joined in on his *nai* with a bright melody, the water in the river gurgled merrily, and the birds in the trees sang along. The girls were so happy – now each had a necklace with both coral and turquoise. They thanked Barzu and wished him a safe trip.

Barzu pedaled off quickly and caught up with Ravshan. They rode and rode along together, pumping their pedals, and came upon a grove of apricot trees where women and children gathered for the harvest. Barzu marveled at all the golden fruit! The boughs were heavy with them and drooped down to the ground. The women gathered apricots from the lower branches, while the children scrambled up to pick them from treetops.

"Hi! Barzu and Ravshan!" the women called. "Are you headed to your grandmother?"

"Yes, we're bringing her a new tanoor," Barzu answered, "so she can bake us her delicious non. You have a big harvest this year, do you need any help?"

"Thank you, Barzu! We definitely need the help. All the men and older kids are working in the watermelon fields. And we want to pick all the apricots before it gets dark."

Barzu grabbed a small bucket and jumped onto an apricot tree. What child does not like to climb trees? All this and he could help people, too. That was double the fun!

In the meantime, Ravshan rested under a tree in the shade. After all, it was hard work towing a tanoor!

The boys only reached their grandmother's house by evening. They brought her new tanoor and a bucket full of apricots, which the women gave them in thanks for their help. Grandmother was so happy to see her grandsons and immediately sat the boys down on the *topchan*, the raised platform in her courtyard, to eat dinner. She made them *plov*, a traditional dish of savory rice and meat, a fresh salad of tomatoes and cucumbers, plus nuts, berries, fresh non, and hot tea. Barzu and Ravshan ate enough to burst!

Their grandmother was so pleased to see such hearty appetites. Her eyes just glowed with joy.

"Grandmother, when will we install the new tanoor?" asked Barzu. "I can't wait to see it!"

"Tomorrow. We will ask our neighbor to help install it. But now it's time to go to sleep," she said, bringing out pillows and some light blankets. "Here, tuck yourselves in comfortably on the topchan. You both must be tired from pedaling all day and gathering so many apricots! Such good boys, always helping people – I am very proud of you! We all have to help each other – it makes life easier and more fun, and everyone can be friends. Working together, we can achieve great things."

"Grandmother, will you tell me a story?" Barzu asked.

"Of course, I will, my little boy."

"How many stories do you know?"

"Many, my dear. I've lived a long time in this world and have heard countless stories and legends. Everything has its own story, its own tale."

"Is there a tale even about non?"

"Even about non."

"Tell me that one!"

The quiet, cool night enveloped the mountains, the valleys, and the villages. Stars lit up the sky and the yellow moon illuminated the courtyard. Ravshan was already soundly asleep but Barzu would never go to sleep without a story from his grandmother. With a kind smile on her face, the old woman began her marvelous tale.

The Bread of Wonder

A long time ago, in a place where great roads crossed, stood the City of Blue Domes, with its narrow, winding streets and the intricate mosaics decorating its high towers. Many different kinds of people lived there and all of the traders and craftsmen, musicians and dancers, the rich and the poor spoke two or three languages so they could understand one another and live together in peace and harmony.

The city was famous for its bazaars where goods were bought and sold.
Oh, and what you could not find there among the stalls! Sweet fruits, crisp
vegetables, clay pots, rare books, fine jewelry, dyed silks, handmade carpets,
leather shoes – everything your heart desired!

And what non they baked there – so aromatic and delicious! The bakers of this city knew the ancient recipe: how to bake non that would not spoil or lose its flavor, not even after three years. Which is why all travelers took this Bread of Wonder with them wherever they went and would never go hungry.

And so, one day, a merchant named Faiz departed the City of Blue Domes with his caravan to far-off Hindustan – the land of rich maharajas, from where he always brought back spices and medicines, pearls, precious stones, and fabulous fabrics. For several months he traveled overland, trekking through the deserts and hills with his caravan of camels, his faithful assistants, and his brave horsemen. Arriving in the City of the Sun, in the Land of Marwar, Faiz immediately made for the fortress towering over a high cliff of red rock, and where the local ruler, Maharaja Sardar, was always ready to welcome traveling merchants.

On this occasion, he found all the streets alive with music, songs, and flowers! Maharaja Sardar had organized a great festival that day to honor the birth of his son. All guests to the fortress were given presents of gold. Everywhere people danced, songs were sung, and poets praised the maharaja and his new heir. The holiday lasted until late at night. Faiz enjoyed himself enormously!

33

The next morning the maharaja invited the merchant for breakfast. Offering his guest to partake of the many fragrant drinks and delicious sweets laid before him, the maharaja asked, "Long it is, since we last saw you in our lands, dear Faiz. How fares your family? How are your children? I trust all is well in your City of Blue Domes?"

"All is well, esteemed Maharaja Sardar," the merchant replied. "Everyone is well and healthy, and our city thrives, as always. I thank you for your concern."

"And have you brought any marvels to divert and amaze me?"

"Indeed, I have, Maharaja Sardar. Please have your servants open my present for you," said Faiz pointing to a wooden trunk that he had brought from far away.

The servants opened the trunk and withdrew from it the round, flat loaves of bread from the City of Blue Domes. But over the six months that they had sat in the trunk, their crusts had become hard as stone.

Taking one in his hand, the maharaja shouted in displeasure, "What is this? What are these bricks you have brought me, Merchant Faiz?"

"This is non from my city," said Faiz with pride. "There is no bread like it anywhere in the world!"

"Are you making fun of me?!" the maharaja asked, his brows furrowed in growing anger. "This bread is so hard, it could break my teeth!"

"I beg you, do not be angry, Your Highness, for these are loaves of the most unusual bread. Please have your servants sprinkle them with water and heat in an oven for two minutes, and then try it once more. I assure you, such bread as this, you have never eaten."

The maharaja had his servants do as Faiz said. They sprinkled water on the bread and placed it in the oven. Two minutes later, they returned the non to the maharaja, only now it was warm, aromatic, and soft. He broke off a piece and placed it in his mouth. Then he took another piece and ate again, and then another piece. He could not stop – the bread was so delicious!

"What is this Bread of Wonder?" the maharaja exclaimed. "Who would believe that this was baked many months ago!"

"I am glad that you are pleased with our bread, O Venerable Maharaja Sardar," the merchant Faiz intoned. "I have brought you forty chests, each filled with loaves of non, so that you may feast on them for many more days to come!"

"Thank you, my friend! Please continue to bring me your miracle from the City of Blue Domes! And because you so surprised and amused me, I shall give you, in return, a box filled with pearls and rubies!"

40

The merchant was happy that he had so delighted the maharaja and he received in return a gift most generous and useful to him in his trade: jewels that could be sold, exchanged for goods, or given again as gifts in his homeland.

This is what happened many, many years ago. To this day, the descendants of those bakers still bake this Bread of Wonder.

"Grandmother, have you ever eaten the Bread of Wonder?" Barzu asked, yawning.

"Of course, I have, my dear. After all, I was born in a city just like that one, with blue domes and intricate mosaics on the walls of its high towers. But now it's time to sleep. May you dream of far-away lands." And she kissed her grandson on his forehead.

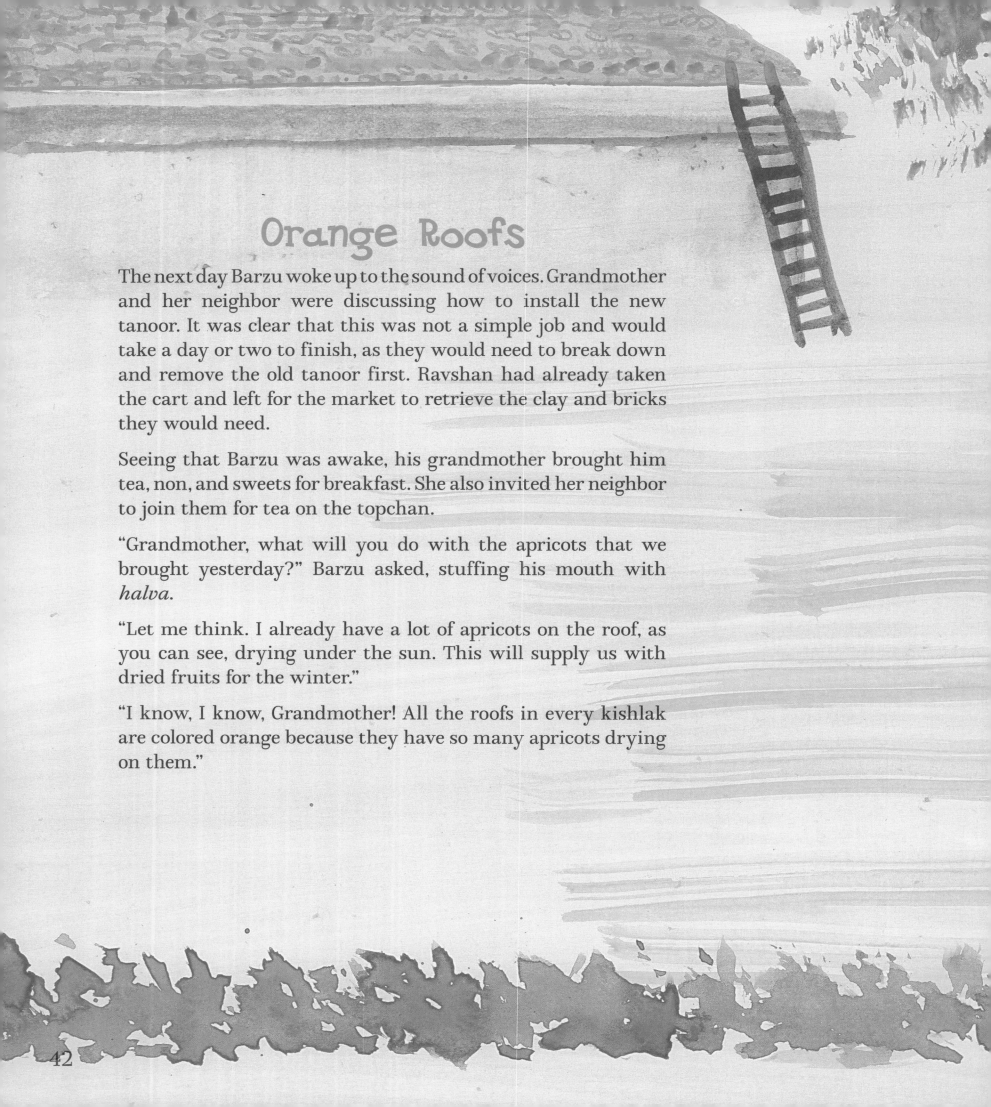

Orange Roofs

The next day Barzu woke up to the sound of voices. Grandmother and her neighbor were discussing how to install the new tanoor. It was clear that this was not a simple job and would take a day or two to finish, as they would need to break down and remove the old tanoor first. Ravshan had already taken the cart and left for the market to retrieve the clay and bricks they would need.

Seeing that Barzu was awake, his grandmother brought him tea, non, and sweets for breakfast. She also invited her neighbor to join them for tea on the topchan.

"Grandmother, what will you do with the apricots that we brought yesterday?" Barzu asked, stuffing his mouth with *halva*.

"Let me think. I already have a lot of apricots on the roof, as you can see, drying under the sun. This will supply us with dried fruits for the winter."

"I know, I know, Grandmother! All the roofs in every kishlak are colored orange because they have so many apricots drying on them."

43

"Yes," the old woman exclaimed, "we truly live on fortunate land! Can you imagine, scientists have found more than 300 different varieties of apricot trees in our region! These trees are so hardy they can withstand drought in summer and the cold of winter. And so, they have taken root here since time immemorial."

"It is good that tourists and scholars sometimes come to stay with you. You feed them your delicious non and they tell you such interesting things," said the neighbor.

"Truly. They tell me and I also tell them. After all, they learn a lot from us, from the old people – the keepers of our ancient knowledge and traditions."

The neighbor nodded his head in full agreement. He had lived his whole life next door to Barzu's grandmother and loved to listen to her stories since he was a child. As he grew up he often came to the old woman for advice and helped her whenever he could. Grandmother often looked after the neighbor's impish children, telling them tales and plying them with tea and sweets.

"Apricots," the old woman continued, "are not just delicious but also healthy fruits, with many important vitamins, which is why we have so many uses for them – we dry them to eat in winter, we make compote and juice, and we produce oil from their seeds. And I know how you love my apricot preserves, Barzu! This reminds me, I have not, yet, prepared any this season so let us use the apricots you brought to make some today. Will you help me?"

"Of course, I will help you, Grandmother! That's easy to make!"

Just then Ravshan returned with the bricks and clay they needed for the new tanoor, and he and the neighbor set right to work. Barzu helped his grandmother remove pits from the apricots. They saved the pits for later when they would also make apricot oil. Barzu would split the pits and remove the tender seeds within and Grandmother would grind the seeds down to let out the oil.

For now, they cut the soft fruit into small pieces, then poured sugar over them in a large bowl and put them aside. They would need to wait a few hours to let the apricot juice merge with the dissolved sugar to create a syrup.

"Do you remember, Barzu, when you were very small, how you climbed into a large bowl filled with apricot syrup and poured it all over yourself? At first, I was so angry, but then I saw how much fun you were having and could not bring myself to scold you. Maybe that's why you're so sweet!" grandmother exclaimed, hugging him warmly.

Barzu laughed. He always enjoyed when she told this story. Secretly, he would have liked to try bathing in the apricot syrup, again, but he was now too big and the bowl too small.

After lunch, Barzu's grandmother boiled the apricots in their syrup to make preserves and then sealed them in jars. On each jar, Barzu glued on a white paper label on which he wrote the word "APRICOTS." Ravshan and the neighbor worked until the evening, taking down the old tanoor and setting up the new one.

And so another day passed on this visit with their grandmother. Before them awaited an entire, hot summer filled with fruits and berries, adventures with friends, and new tales about the City of Blue Domes.

The Secrets of Master Zafar

Zafar, master of his craft! He builds his tanoors from an ancient recipe, preserved in his family since time immemorial. All of the men in his family, from generation to generation, were tanoor-masters: his father, and his grandfather, and his great-grandfather, and his great-great-grandfather, and his great-great-great-grandfather.

great-great-great-
grandfather

great-great-grand-
father

great-grandfather

grandfather

father

Zafar

Making tanoors is hard and laborious work, requiring a lot of patience, and Zafar always does his best. He is helped by his sons and a few apprentices.

First, the master sends his apprentices off in different directions to find the best quality yellow clay, red clay, and brown clay and bring it all back to the workshop. Then, they must mix the three types of clay together, adding wool from sheep or goats, straw, rice husks, and water.

What do they need the wool for? It is an ancient secret! Wool helps the tanoor last longer and keep the heat in better. The straw binds the mixture together perfectly and the rice husks add extra insulation.

From early morning to late at night, the apprentices knead this mixture with their bare feet, tramping over it until it turns into a soft, blended mass, like dough. Sometimes for fun, Barzu likes to jump onto the clay himself and hop around making faces, which amuses his father.

Once this careful mixing is done, Zafar stores the clay in a cool place. After a few days, he or an apprentice will pull off large chunks of clay, first kneading them by hand into round logs and then flattening them out with their feet into ribbons. He sprinkles ash over the logs so his feet won't stick to the clay. The ribbons of clay are left in the shade for another twenty four hours and then taken by Zafar to sculpt with various tools into a beautiful tanoor.

When finished, the tanoor will have a shape like a jar or bell. It may be large or small, more round in shape or more oval. The tanoor will be left in the sun to dry, where it will remain for no less than three days.

It is common in Central Asia for the buyer and seller to haggle over the price. Upon agreement and payment, Zafar will deliver the oven to the buyer's home and also install it. To do so, he first builds a small fireplace out of masonry or slotted bricks that allow the air to flow under the stove, which will help the fire burn better. Next, he will stand the tanoor vertically over the fireplace with its neck up, finally covering it all under a thick layer of clay and bricks.

Many people, such as Barzu's grandmother, prefer to mount their ovens horizontally, which is called a "front-facing" tanoor. For this, they build

a base out of brick against a wall. They pour a bed of sand onto the base to hold and insulate the oven and then lay the tanoor on top. Finally, they enclose the tanoor in bricks and a thick layer of clay, leaving a hole in the upper wall of the oven as a vent. Here the fire is lit inside the tanoor, rather than in the fireplace below.

Sometimes Master Zafar is asked to make a tanoor all out of brick. These are very strong and large tanoors that are usually needed in the bazaar or *chaikhana*, where they must bake a thousand non a day to sell to their customers.

Travel to the World of Barzu!

Dear travelers! Yes, that is what we call all of you who have read this book because to be a traveler you do not have to pack your bags and head to foreign lands. Books, just like trains, planes, and boats, can transport us to different countries and introduce us to new faces and cultures. Books can let you have adventures, show you both funny and sad things, teach you about the past, and help you see the future.

Travelers are also very curious. They think everything is interesting – their own home, their street, their city, the whole planet, and even outer space! Just like you do. Real travelers explore their world. They like to see, taste, and try everything for themselves.

You have learned a lot of new things in this book! And you can keep exploring with this travel guide to Barzu's world. Let's go, our caravan is heading out!

First stop: Take two sets of beads with different colors (maybe one with red beads and one with blue, just as in the story). Make necklaces of one color each, and then mix them up to make two necklaces with both colors. If you don't have beads, you can try buttons, cut up pieces of drinking straws, or even painted macaroni.

Second stop: Make your own tanoor and non out of clay or Play Doh. See what they look like in the book for reference.

Third stop: Find a map of the world and locate the countries of Central Asia: Kazakhstan, Kyrgyzstan, Tajikistan, Turkmenistan, Uzbekistan.

Fourth stop: Imagine that, just 100 years ago, there were no telephones, no television, no computers, and no internet. How do you think people got information? How did they learn about important events or different parts of the world? Maybe parents know the answer to these questions!

Fifth stop: Do you want to taste what Barzu eats for lunch? You can find *plov*, *samsa*, and *non* in the menu of any Tajik or Uzbek restaurant. Can you find this kind of restaurant near you? If so, you may even be able to see a real tanoor there – some restaurants have them.

Sixth stop: Make your own apricot compote or preserves. Compote is a drink made from boiling fruits, rather than squeezing them. You just need to put apricots, water, and sugar in a big pot – bring it to the boil, then turn it off and let it cool. That's it! The compote will be even better if you add other fruits and berries such as apples, pears, and cherries. You already know how to prepare preserves from the chapter "Orange Roofs."

Seventh stop: Have you ever tasted dried apricots? If not, you can find them in a supermarket. This is a sweet and healthy snack you can eat anywhere – while hiking, in school, even on the beach.

Eighth stop: Let's bake real non! I have four wonderful recipes for you.

Mai Tokoch

Kyrgyz: "Bread on Oil"

Ingredients:

1 teaspoon active dry yeast
3 cups flour (sifted)
1 cup warm milk
1 egg
1 tablespoon vegetable oil
$1/2$ teaspoon salt
$1/2$ teaspoon sugar (if desired)
butter or vegetable oil

In a bowl, dissolve the yeast in warmed milk, then blend in the egg, salt, and sugar. Add the flour and knead into dough.

Cover the dough, preferably wrapping the entire bowl in a towel, and place in a warm spot to rise for about an hour. After an hour, uncover the dough and carefully push the risen dough back down, pressing with your fist to flatten it. Cover and leave to rise for another hour. Remove the dough onto a lightly floured surface. Divide the dough into four to six pieces, depending on the size of your frying pan.

Turn the pieces into balls and then roll each piece out into a circle no more than one centimeter (less than half an inch) in width. Cut three slits into the center of each circle.

Mai Tokoch is usually fried in a special butter unique to the region but for home use, any type of butter or vegetable oil will do. Add the butter or oil to the pan over medium heat and then fry each piece of dough on both sides until golden brown. *Mai Tokoch* is light and airy, and looks delicious.

Zagora

**Orange non
made from corn flour**

Ingredients:

$1/2$ teaspoon active dry yeast
2 $1/2$ cups corn flour
$1/2$ cup warm milk
$3/4$ cup grated pumpkin or carrot
$1/3$ cup finely chopped tomatoes
$1/3$ cup finely chopped red bell pepper
$1/3$ cup finely chopped onion
5-6 tablespoons vegetable oil (or 150 grams/
5 ounces of melted butter/margarine)
1 teaspoon salt
$1/2$ teaspoon sugar (if desired)

This is a good, gluten-free recipe! Grate the pumpkin on a medium grater. Finely chop onion, pepper, and tomatoes, and then mix with pumpkin and salt in a bowl. In a separate bowl, dissolve the yeast in warmed milk, then add the oil/butter and flour. Add the vegetables to the mix and knead. The dough should not be too hard or too soft. If it falls apart in your hand, let the dough sit for about 30 minutes in a warm place and then test to see if it has become less crumbly. The vegetables should add juice over that time, helping the dough become more "sticky." If it is still too crumbly, add a little bit of milk.

Cover the dough, preferably by wrapping the entire bowl in a towel, and store in a warm place for about two hours. Once it has risen to about double or triple in size, turn it onto a lightly floured surface and separate into six to eight pieces. Grease the pan with margarine or vegetable oil. Knead pieces of dough into balls and then flatten down to a width of no more than 1.5 centimeters (a little over half an inch). The dough for *zagora* is delicate and can fall apart in your hands, so it is better to place the balls onto the pan, first, and then knead and flatten them.

Bake in the oven at 220°C (420°F) until the crust turns reddish-gold. This bright orange bread is best served hot with sour cream on the side.

Noni Tova	Non
Tajik: "Non on the Pan"	

Ingredients:

1 cup warm milk
100 grams/5 ounces melted margarine or butter
1 teaspoon salt (or less, per taste)
$^1/_2$ teaspoon sesame or nigella seeds
2-3 cups flour

Ingredients:

1 tablespoon active dry yeast
4 $^1/_2$ cups sifted flour
$^1/_2$ tablespoon salt
$^1/_2$ tablespoon sugar

Mix milk, margarine, salt, and the sesame seeds together in a bowl. Add two cups of flour and mix well. If the dough can be easily kneaded into a ball, then it is ready. If too soft or moist, add more flour. Cover dough and leave in a warm place for 30 minutes. Turn onto a lightly floured surface, divide the dough into 6-7 pieces, knead them into balls, and then flatten them into circles so they are approximately 1 centimeter thick (less than half an inch) and 10 centimeters (about 4 inches) in diameter. You can add patterns to the dough with a fork.

Heat the frying pan, place the circles, cover with a lid, and reduce heat. You do not need to grease the pan as there is already enough oil or margarine in the dough. Turn the bread over after about a minute, or whenever the bottom turns golden-brown, and cover again. Once the second side turns brown, the bread is ready!

Bring two cups of water to boil. Pour one and a half cups into a large bowl. Add salt, sugar and stir until they dissolve. Let the water cool (approximately 5–7 minutes). Add first the yeast, stir well, and then add the flour. If the dough seems too stiff, add water. Knead the dough for about 20–30 minutes so that it is soft but does not stick to your hands. Cover dough and store it in a warm place for two hours.

Divide the dough into two to four parts. Knead them into large balls and place them in a greased pan. To give the bread its special shape, stretch the dough with your fingers from the center outward to make the center thinner and the edges thicker. You can rub the dough with milk and either sesame seeds, egg yolk, or kefir diluted with water to give the crust a golden color.

The temperature and cooking time depends on your oven. A gas oven should be heated to 220°C/420°F and the *non* baked for 30 minutes. For electric ovens, heat to 190°C/380°F; after the first 15 minutes, you will need to check the bread every 5–10 minutes.

Non can be eaten with sour cream, butter, soup, or just as it is – this bread will come out surprisingly delicious and filling!

Ethnographic Notes

(Illustrations by the author)

When I decided to write my series of books *The World of Barzu*, I wanted, first and foremost, to tell children about the countries of Central Asia. Each of these countries is beautiful and unique in its own way, but they are also closely linked by a shared history and culture, which are still alive in their customs and traditions, languages, handicrafts, and cooking. That is why, although Barzu and his family live in the mountains of Tajikistan, their lifestyle is very similar to the other, historically sedentary peoples of Central Asia.

Nothing in Central Asia is as simple as it first looks. I hope that my ethnographic findings will help young readers and their parents learn and appreciate the amazing diversity of this region. Please note that this is not a textbook or a scientific paper, rather it is just a starting point, a seed of information. It is up to you to decide whether this seed can grow into a tree that can feed your curiosity in a long and fascinating journey around the world.

Central Asia

We begin with the name for the region. What is Central Asia, where is it and what countries are found there? As strange as it seems, there is no single answer.

In 1978, the United Nations Educational, Scientific, and Cultural Organization (UNESCO) defined the region as the "territories lying at present within the boundaries of Afghanistan, the western part of China, northern India, north-eastern Iran, Mongolia, Pakistan and the Central Asian Republics of the Union of Soviet Socialist Republics (USSR)".

In Russian, the older term *Srednyaya Aziya*, meaning "Middle Asia," typically designated the lands of the settled peoples in what are now Kyrgyzstan, Tajikistan, Turkmenistan, and Uzbekistan, sometimes including and sometimes excluding the vast Kazakh steppe lands.

In this book, I focus on the five countries of Kazakhstan, Kyrgyzstan, Tajikistan, Turkmenistan, and Uzbekistan. This corresponds with the countries' own contemporary designation of their region as Central Asia.

What Do the Countries of Central Asia Have in Common?

The countries of Central Asia received their modern borders only about one hundred years ago. For centuries before then, the many peoples there

lived side by side, interacted, and developed together. Commonly, they were differentiated not by ethnicity but by way of life or occupation: sedentary farmers, artisans, merchants, and nomads.

In this region are found some of the oldest cities in the world: Andijan, Bukhara, Istarafshan, Kokand, Khiva, Khujand, Merv, Osh, Samarkand, and Shakhrisabz, all of which are more than two thousand years old. States and civilizations arose time and again and then collapsed, due to economic problems or the strains of constant war.

Between the 2nd century B.C. to the 15th century A.D., Central Asia played an important role in the Silk Road — the series of trade routes carrying caravans of merchants between Asia and Europe. Cities were founded and grew rich along these routes, becoming influential centers where news and technology could be exchanged, and where cultures and religions spread. For example, Europeans learned about gunpowder and paper from the Chinese, brought to them from the Silk Road.

Fertile lands and rich cities have always attracted the ambitions of world conquerors. Alexander the Great, Genghis Khan, and Tamerlane are all

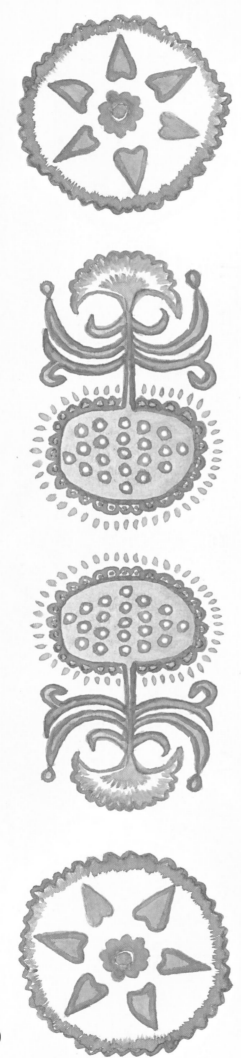

names that evoked terror and awe in their time. These three military leaders changed the course of world history, and their destinies are all tied to Central Asia.

Alexander the Great

The young King Alexander of Macedon, having already conquered all of Greece, set out east in 334 B.C. and defeated Darius III, who ruled the Persian Achaemenid Empire. He then moved on in 329 B.C. to subdue Margiana, Bactria, and Sogdiana – lands that now make up Tajikistan, Turkmenistan, and Uzbekistan, but once were part of the Achaemenid Empire. After two or three years of fierce fighting, Alexander conquered the largest cities, even renaming some of them or founding new ones in his own honor. One such city was *Alexandria Eskhata* ("Alexandria the Farthest" in Greek), now called Khujand in Tajikistan. Alexander's conquest of Central Asia brought Greek influence into the East and Eastern goods and thought into the West. Many historians see this as the start of the Silk Road.

Names and titles change in different languages, and so Alexander's name became al-Iskandar in Arabic. He was also called Iskander Zulkarnain (or Dulkarnai), which means, "two-horned." Why did they call him that? According to one legend, Alexander the Great had two horns on his head, carefully hidden behind long curls. Some historians think it is a metaphor for his conquering the two "horns" of the world – the West (Europe) and the East (Asia).

Two thousand years have since passed but the people of Central Asia tell legends and folktales about Iskander to this day. There are brave souls exploring caves in Turkmenistan and Uzbekistan, in search of treasure allegedly abandoned by Macedonian scouts. One of the most beautiful high-mountainous lakes in Tajikistan – Iskanderkul ("Lake Iskander" in Tajik) – is named in honor of the great general. According to legend, the army of Alexander the Great halted to rest by the shores of this lake, where Alexander's favorite horse, Bucephalus, is said to have tripped into the water and drowned. Since that time, they say that on full moons the waters of the lake part and a white horse emerges to graze along the shore.

The Yazguli, a people living in Tajikistan's Pamir Mountains, also have a story to tell of al-Iskandar. They claim that it was there, on the bank of the Yazgulam River, that Alexander found his death at the hands of the brave warrior Andar, and was buried there, in the Pamirs. To this day, they say that on the anniversary of his death the river waters turn red. The mountain settlement of Andarbag was named in Andar's honor.

Genghis Khan

Fifteen centuries later, Central Asia became part of another empire, this time led by the world-conquering Genghis Khan. The Great Mongol Empire was the largest land empire in history, encompassing China, Central Asia, most of modern Russia, the Caucasus, Eastern Europe, Iran, and Afghanistan.

The army of Genghis Khan and his sons destroyed many of the ancient trade centers of Central Asia. The great city Otrar, at that time one of the largest and most developed cities in the region (in what is now Kazakhstan), was completely demolished and deserted after a six-month siege. For several centuries, the gleaming centers of Samarkand, Bukhara, and Khujand lay in ruins after Mongol invasions, and once-powerful Merv (in modern-day Turkmenistan) would never restore its former greatness. The subjugation of the great oasis cities allowed the Mongols to launch further invasions to the west and to the north.

However, after the territories were conquered, new cities were built, trade was re-established, and merchants once again led their caravans along the Silk Road. Genghis Khan and his heirs created a great expanse of peace and trade from Europe to Asia – an era called the *Pax Mongolica* (Latin for "Mongol Peace"). They introduced courier postal service, sophisticated use of military intelligence, and brought the paper money invented by the Chinese into widespread use. The Mongol empire was also noteworthy for its tolerance of different religions.

The Great Mongol Empire lasted for only 150 years. It fell apart in the 14th century but even afterwards, right up until the early 20th century, all of Central Asia's succeeding rulers claimed descent directly from Genghis Khan to legitimize their rule. To this day you will find boys across the region named Chingiz (Genghis) in honor of the great Khan. People believe that the name endows strength, intelligence, and courage.

Tamerlane

In 1336, in a settlement near Shahrisabz, in modern-day Uzbekistan, a boy was born named Timur, meaning "Iron." The son of the chief of an insignificant Turkic-speaking tribe, the "iron" boy grew up to create

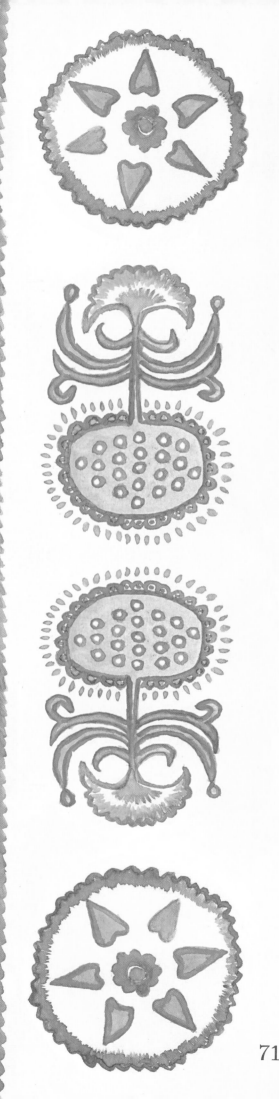

a vast empire stretching from the Chinese border to the Mediterranean Sea, with Samarkand as his capital.

Timur's ferocious army brought terror to people everywhere, fully destroying whole cities, and taking hundreds of thousands of people into slavery. During one of his unrelenting battles, Timur was seriously wounded in his leg and afterward walked with a pronounced limp. Because of this, he came to be called in Persian *Timur-i-Lang*, or "Timur the Lame", which in Europe is pronounced "Tamerlane."

World history judges Tamerlane as a formidable and ruthless conqueror but he is also remembered for the beautiful architecture he inspired. The renowned Timurid style is striking in its variety of forms and grace and widely influential across the East.

Having brought destruction to other countries, Tamerlane sought to rebuild his own capital Samarkand so that its beauty and immensity would outshine all other cities in the world. By his order, aqueducts and roads were built, vast gardens and vineyards flourished, and great mosques, palaces, and mausoleums decorated the skyline.

What is so special about this? Had no one else done this before? Domes, palaces, towers, and minarets could be found everywhere, and gardens were always important in Islam, representing the ideals of paradise. What was different is that, in Tamerlane's ambition to portray himself as the founder of a new world, he built on a scale not seen before. His gardens were so vast that, it is said, a horse that got lost in one would not be found for six months. The mighty domes stretching upward with their deep turquoise tiles seemed to rule over the stars. The glaze tile designs covering so much of the inner and outer walls of Tamerlane's buildings surpassed anything that came before in intricacy and color.

Tamerlane's whole approach was innovative for its day. From his conquered territories, he brought in not just hundreds of thousands of captive slaves, but also thousands of high-skilled architects, artists, and craftsmen to realize his ideas. Enslaved artisans streamed into Samarkand from Damascus, Tabriz, Baghdad, Shiraz, Isfahan, Delhi, the cities of the Caucasus and from across Central Asia. They all came from diverse architectural and artistic traditions and each brought his own unique skills. In this way, Samarkand became a kind of creative laboratory, in which craftsmen experimented on new methods, technologies, building styles, and ornamentation. They used cutting-edge technologies for that era, and they were given the best materials to work with, from Tamerlane's unlimited resources of marble, onyx, precious stones, and gold. Out of this laboratory with diverse influences emerged a unified style that had not been seen before and that would become a wonder of the world.

Even after six centuries, the surviving creations of Tamerlane's architects, from the Shah-i-Zinda ensemble to Bibi-Khanym Mosque and Gur-i-Amir (Gur-Emir), attest to the past glory of Samarkand. The majestic towers and domes, glittering tiles, the enchanting majolica mosaic ornaments, carved marble, the murals made with gold and lapis lazuli – all this leaves an unforgettable impression on anyone fortunate enough to behold them.

But Samarkand was not the only focus of the ruler's attention. Tamerlane encouraged the same in other cities – in Bukhara and Yassy (modern Turkestan), Kesh (modern Shahrisabz), and elsewhere, you can find even more examples of his architecture. More than empire, his legacy was in the craftsmen, who continued to build and to teach their apprentices, who would then move on to other rich patrons in new cities, thereby contributing to the spread of the Timurid style across Asia.

The Soviet Union

Over the course of the 1800s, Russian imperial forces conquered more and more Central Asian land, absorbing the Kazakh steppe, Kyrgyz mountain-pastures, the Turkmen deserts, and the emirates of Bukhara, Ferghana, and Kokand. All of these lands were administered by the Turkestan General-Governorship, with its capital in Tashkent.

However, the Russian Empire itself was soon engulfed in a revolution, leading to the end of the monarchy in 1917, a bloody civil war, and the creation of the Union of Soviet Socialist Republics (USSR) in 1922, which included the Turkestan Autonomous Soviet Socialist Republic (ASSR).

The Soviet government broke the Turkestan ASSR up in the 1920s, for a variety of political and administrative reasons, and created new republics that now make up the independent countries of Kazakhstan, Kyrgyzstan, Tajikistan, Turkmenistan, and Uzbekistan. The republics were meant as national homelands for the five primary ethnic and linguistic groups in the region – Kazakhs, Kyrgyz, Tajiks, Turkmens, and Uzbeks – but the process of creating new borders was messy and inconsistent and still has impacts to this day.

Over the 70 years of the Soviet Union's existence, Central Asia also saw the massive arrival of diverse ethnic groups from other parts of the country due to labor migration, deportations, and evacuations from the front during the Second World War. In 1991, the Soviet Union collapsed and all five states gained independence.

The Ethnic and Linguistic Diversity of Central Asia

Due to this complex history, and particularly the legacy of the Soviet era, dozens of ethnic groups live in every country of Central Asia. Kazakhstan alone boasts over a hundred different ethnic groups. Uzbeks can be found in Kazakhstan, Kyrgyzstan, Tajikistan, and Turkmenistan. You can find Kyrgyz yurts in Tajikistan, and Tajik farmers in Kyrgyzstan. On the Kazakh border with China, there lives an ethnic group called Uighurs.

It is not surprising that we can recognize the ancient cities of Bukhara and Samarkand in the tale Barzu's grandmother tells of the City of Blue Domes. These cities in Uzbekistan are an inseparable part of history not just for the Uzbeks but for other ethnicities, particularly the Tajiks. For example, according to the 1897 census in Samarkand, under the Russian Empire, there were 5,506 Uzbek speakers and 35,845 Tajik speakers, whereas residents outside the city mostly spoke Uzbek. The census of that year also registered Armenian, Russian, Kashgari, Tatar, and Persian speakers, as well as speakers of Bukhori, the language of Central Asian Jews. So, for centuries, an average Samarkand resident could speak at least two or more languages, an ordinary occurrence throughout Central Asia. Even today it is common to hear Tajik in these cities. Both Uzbek and Tajik citizens have family living across the border.

The native languages of Central Asia belong to two different families: the Indo-European and the Altaic. Here, Kazakh, Kyrgyz, Turkmen, Uzbek, Uighur, and Karakalpak all fall under the Turkic branch of the Altaic language family. And the Tajik language (one of the Persian languages), as well as Vakhan, Yazgulyam, Shugnan, Yagnob, Ishkashim, Rushan, and Bartang, are all part of the Iranian group of the Indo-European language family. Each language also divides into different dialects. Russian is used as a common tongue and is frequently spoken in most cities, as it became widespread during the Soviet years.

The Wondrous Oven

The clay oven is one of humanity's most ancient inventions. Scholars believe that the *tanoor* first appeared thousands of years ago in ancient Sumeria and Akkadia, in the region the Greeks called Mesopotamia, and then spread from there to other lands. That is why we find clay ovens not only in Central Asia but also in Armenia, China, Egypt, Georgia, India, Iraq, Iran, Japan, Pakistan, Syria, and Turkey.

There are many different types of clay found in nature, and many different colors: white, brown, gray-brown, gray, almost black, red, green, blue and yellow. Clay is important for its plasticity (its ability to be shaped into different forms) and its resistance to fire and water. It also has unique antibacterial characteristics and health benefits as it is saturated with iron, potassium, calcium, magnesium, zinc, copper, and other minerals. Noticing all these wonderful properties of clay, ancient people began to use it in many ways. They made ovens and kitchenware, containers for food and drink, they built and decorated their houses with clay, and used it for medicine and cosmetics.

In Central Asia, both men and women make *tanoors*, since men often went to war or had to work far away. In the book you learned about Master Zafar's secrets for building *tanoors* but, in fact, there are many ways to build one, depending on local techniques and what materials are available in nature. So, for example, Uighurs in southeast Kazakhstan build the *tanoor* from ten narrow strips of yellow clay, adding one strip per day over ten days. Compare this with the two to three strips of clay that Master Zafar used over just a few days. Interestingly, in some places, the Uighurs feed small amounts of yellow clay to their children in the spring, as they believe the minerals and vitamins help nourish young bodies in need of nutrients after winter. They call these "clay cookies."

Tanoor makers may add different types of animal hair to the clay, from the goat or sheep wool that Master Zafar uses, to camel's wool or even the hair from a cow's tail. The inner walls of some *tanoors* may be lined with small rocks and the outer walls with large ones.

We see in the story how *tanoors* are often made for sale and delivery but many people will also build their own at home. Some households will have more than one: perhaps a vertically standing oven, a front-facing one, and a small tanoor called *degdón* or *degdonchá* that is used as a stove.

In certain communities, *tanoors* are almost entirely underground, and the people there will call it *chakhlák*. In the Pamir mountains, *tanoors* in many homes are built into a raised platform along the wall and are called *kitsór* or *ardón*. After cooking, people will then place a board and rugs over the platform to make a warm nook for sitting or sleeping on in winter.

What else can you cook in a *tanoor* besides non? In Central Asia, you can cook delicious *samsá* or *samboosá* – little pastries filled with something good, most often meat or pumpkin. People also cook meat in *tanoors*, hanging it over the neck of a vertical *tanoor* by a metal skewer. If you are using a small *degdón* (*deg* – cauldron, *don* – stand), you can cook the meat in a large pot with potatoes, or with rice to make delicious *plov* (pilaf).

The word *tanoor* that I use in this book is based on one of the more common words found in Tajikistan. But this stove is called many things by many people in different dialects and languages. In Tajikistan alone, there are more than 10 different names: *tandoor, tandýr, chagdón, otashdón, oshtón, chavlák, chalák, chakhlák, kitsór, ardón, degdón, degdoon, dedón*. In Turkmenistan, it is called a *tamdír* and the Uighurs of Kazakhstan call it a *tonoor*.

English speakers are most familiar with the word *tandoor*, which comes from the Indian version of the oven, and *tandoori nan* or *tandoori bread* are common menu items in Indian restaurants.

Koolchái Kalón

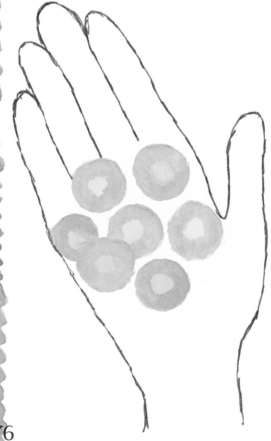

Koolchái Choí

The Bread of Wonder

Anyone who has been to Samarkand, even just once, has tried its famous bread! At the local market, at any time of day or night, dozens of vendors will offer you their freshly baked *non*, which really does last a long time without spoiling, just as in the story. What a wonder! People pass on tales about rulers from other cities who loved Samarkand's bread and wished to have it made the same way. *Tanoor* masters and bakers were brought from Samarkand to recreate the recipes but they could not, as if it was the Samarkand air, sun, and water that made the bread so special.

In Central Asia, bread is called *non* or *nan*. For centuries, the round *non* was revered as a symbol of the sun and of fertility. As a rule, *non* is not cut with a knife, rather the oldest member of the family or a guest to one's house tears it into pieces by hand. Children are taught to respect bread and pick up even the smallest crumbs from the floor. In one custom, travelers would eat a piece of bread before a long journey and their family would keep the rest of the loaf in a secure place, to guarantee his safe return. And during Tajik weddings, the groom's mother, while offering her good wishes, may pull apart a whole *non* over the bride's head, as the future keeper of the family hearth.

Bread is such an important part of people's life in Central Asia, that this staple food is called by well over 150 different names, depending on the city, region, or country it is made, or what time of day it is baked, how it is baked, and what recipe is used. The dough can be flaky, spongy, it can be sourdough or sweet, it can taste buttery or salty. Bakers may add sour milk, fruit, nuts, butter, broth, herbs, vegetables, or meat to the recipe. Bread may be small, like a cookie, large like a plate, or enormous – up to one meter (three feet) in diameter. Bread may be baked in a *tanoor* or in an oven, it can be fried on the stove, and some will bake the dough directly in hot ashes or sand. It can take as little as one minute to bake *non* or it can take hours. There is everyday bread and there is bread baked for special occasions.

Here are some examples that show the diversity of bread across Central Asia:

Fatíri Goongák (Tajikistan)
The Tajik translates literally as "Dumb Fatir." The dough for fatíri goongák is made from the black flour of a local sort of wheat. No yeast is added and the bread comes out quite hard and well-suited for a dish of *koorootób*. Residents of Muminabad in southern Tajikistan joke that a blow on the head with this bread can knock you speechless. According to the recipe for *koorootób*, the fatíri goongák is placed in a bowl, soaked in a mixture of hot water and fermented milk called *chakká*, and smothered in fresh curds and vegetables. The bread will soak up the flavor but soften only gradually.

Galá Osiyó (Uzbekistan)
The very Bread of Wonders from our story! Once, over seventy flour mills stood on the banks of the river Obi-Rahmat, on the outskirts of Samarkand, and the whole city would go there to have their wheat ground into

flour. It was also where the most delicious bread was baked. This area was called Galá Osiyó, which in Persian means "Many Mills." The mills are no longer there but the name and the secrets of baking, together with the special air and water of Samarkand, remain.

Fatíri Ará-Ará (Tajikistan)
An enormous flatbread, baked to celebrate engagements and weddings. It is decorated with the help of a saw, *ará* in Tajik.

Kadilí Chorék (Turkmenistan, Uzbekistan)
Pumpkin bread – ground pumpkin (*kadí* in Turkmen) is added with milk to the dough. It is worth noting that both the words *nan* and *chorek* are used for bread in Turkmenistan. Kadili chorek is baked in the *tanoor* and comes out with a bright orange sheen.

Gommé Chorék (Turkmenistan)
In Turkmen, this means "buried bread." Gommé chorék is traditionally baked by shepherds in the Kara-Kum desert. First, they kindle a bonfire, then they remove the coal, and dig a pit about 15-20 centimeters deep (about 5-7 inches) into the heated sand. They place the dough into the pit and bury it in the sand, rekindle the fire, and an hour and a half later chorék is ready. The hot sand does not stick to the dough and the slow-cooked bread will not mold, so shepherds can store it in their bags for a long time.

Kombésh Nan (Kazakhstan)
Also "buried bread" but this time in the Kazakh language. To make it, you place the dough onto a large frying pan, then cover the pan and place *kizyák* above and below (see more information about *kizyak* on p.88). The bread will bake through top to bottom.

Chap-Chak (Tajikistan, Uzbekistan)
Chap-chak is a crispy, puffed bread baked in a *tanoor*. It makes a delicious breakfast, served hot with sour cream, grapes, or melon.

Óbi Nahood (Nahood Non) (Tajikistan, Uzbekistan)
Families will often soak chickpeas in water for other meals, particularly *plov* or *shurpo*, but instead of throwing the water away, they will use it to make the dough for this bread – *ob* means "water" and *nahood* are peas. The peas are soaked in the water for 8–10 hours and then the baker uses this water to make non, which lends the bread a special flavor. The water also gives the bread a beautiful, shiny sheen, making this a popular bread for weddings.

Tagaloví (Tajikistan)
This word means "under the fire" in Tajik. To maximize space in the *tanoor*, once the walls have been covered in baking *non*, the baker will place one more ball of dough between two flat rocks and bury it under the ash at the bottom of the oven for 40 minutes. This manner of baking changes the name of the bread, although it is made from the exact same dough as the others baked on the walls. Sometimes nuts, raisins, dried apricots, or other ingredients are added to tagaloví.

Chalpák (Tajikistan, Uzbekistan)
Thin flatbreads fried in oil, in a cauldron. In Tajikistan, people will offer

chalpáks to their friends, family, and neighbors when a child is born. Also called *chelpék* or *shelpék* in other parts of Central Asia.

Zabóni Gov (Tajikistan, Uzbekistan)
"Cow Toungue" in Tajik, so named because of its oblong shape, unlike most other, round *non*.

Satrí (Tajikistan)
A rich, fluffy bread decorated with elaborate designs, usually baked for weddings or for the spring equinox festival of Navruz. Satrí are usually cooked after standard *non* have been baked in the *tanoor*; once they are taken out, the bread makers will place a grill over the still-hot ashes and then place a baking tray over it with the prepared dough. They will cover the top of the *tanoor* with a lid, wrap the *tanoor* in blankets and leave the bread to bake for several hours, sometimes overnight. Sealing the *tanoor* keeps the heat in for a long time, allowing the bread to slow-cook. The word *satr* in Tajik means "to cover" or "to close."

Goozapayagí (Tajikistan, Uzbekistan)
Bread baked in a *tanoor* fired by the stem of cotton plants, rather than wood or, more commonly today, gas. The stems, called *goozapayá*, give the bread a unique taste and aroma. Cotton is cultivated in much of Uzbekistan and the lowlands of Tajikistan.

Naabái Nan (Kyrgyzstan)
This is what they call *non* baked fresh and sold in the bazaars in Kyrgyzstan, as opposed to *ui non*, "homemade" non. *Naabai* means "baker" in Kyrgyz and is similar to *novvói* or *nonvói* in Uzbekistan and Tajikistan. It is very common to name bread after the place where it was made. So, for example, *Ulugbek non* is bread made near the Ulugbek Observatory in Samarkand.

Pooshták (Pooshtá Non) (Tajikistan, Uzbekistan)
Pooshtak translates as "the one that comes after." Sometimes a bread maker makes more dough than needed. Let's say a mid-sized *tanoor* can bake ten *non* but you have made enough dough for thirteen *non*. Right after those first ten *non* have baked, you place the last three in the *tanoor*. The oven is now less hot than before so the bread will bake more slowly. Even though the dough is the same as the others, the longer baking time over less heat makes the pooshtak come out firmer, crunchier (which children love) and with a slightly different taste. Pooshtak is particularly good in *shorpá*, a thick meat soup. And if a *non* falls off the oven wall into the ash while still raw, the bread maker will turn it over and stick it back on to finish baking, as wasting bread is a sin in Central Asia. This kind of *non* is called *doopooshtá*, or a bread "with two backs."

Joosái Nan (Kazakhstan, Kyrgyzstan)
This type of flatbread comes from the Uighurs, an ethnic group found primarily in China, but with significant minorities in Kazakhstan and Kyrgyzstan, and also found in other parts of Central Asia. Uighurs add *joosai*, a green onion called "fragrant-flowered garlic" in English or "Chinese chives" (scientific name *Allium ramosum*), to the dough and then fry the flat cakes in a pan. The aromatic *joosai* gives the bread a sweet-smell-

ing, garlic-onion flavor. Uighurs and Dungans, another ethnic group, prepare numerous dishes with *joosai*, including *lagman* (noodle stew) and *manti* (dumplings), a distinctive and unforgettable part of their cooking.

The people in the larger cities of Uzbekistan and Tajikistan are particularly proud of their own, locally-made, bread. The *non* from Bukhara, or Dushanbe, Kokand or Khujand, Samarkand or Tashkent, all taste and look differently, and are decorated distinctively from one another.

Additionally, the same bread can have the same name across the region but with different pronunciations. So, for example, a non with flaky, buttery dough can be called, variously, *katlamá*, *gatlamá*, or *kalamá*. *Fatír* can be called *patýr*, *petír*, *batýr*, or *batyér*.

Feathers, Spoons, Forks, and Keys

The patterns and designs on each *non*, like a secret telegram, can tell you who baked it and where, and for what occasion. Every city and region has its own traditional patterns pressed into the dough. Every single baker and home-maker has them, too. The designs are set into the dough in many ways: with special stamps, or with spoons, knives and forks, with fingers, keys, teacups, ram's bones, combs, or wood-saws. Yes, even saws! What won't people think of! It turns out that saws are very good for decorating *koolchái kalón* or *fatíri ará-ará*, which are large *non* reaching a whole meter (three feet) in diameter.

Sesame seeds and colored rice may also be used to decorate the bread. Most often, however, the *non* will be sprinkled with aromatic *Nigella sativa* seeds (also known as kalijeera, black caraway, or black cumin). In Central Asia, this spice is called *sédoná* which comes from the Persian *siyáh donéh* ("black seed").

Do you remember how Barzu's grandmother used a tool called a *nonpar* to decorate her bread? *Par* in Persian means "feather" because, originally, people would use a bunch of rooster feathers to make their designs. And just as with the bread itself, this decorative instrument is called by many different names across all the corners of Central Asia.

In Kyrgyzstan, it is called *chekích, chekchí*, or *chakách*. In Uzbekistan, it may be a *bezhák, chekích, chakoosh, chakích, chakshí, chakkí, chkich, nonpár (nanpar, nampar), tikách, tkach, tkech, tikésh*, or *tikóch*. In Turkmenistan, they say *tikéch* or *doortgooch*. In Kazakhstan, they use the words *chekích, chakooch, chakoosh, shekísh*, or *dookkí*.

I was able to compile twenty completely different names for this instrument in Tajikistan alone (though I am sure there are more!). This diversity in names reflects the country's mountainous geography, which covers ninety three percent of its territory, where high mountains isolate communities from one another. In addition, the people living in the Pamir Mountains were secluded for so long by the surrounding peaks that, to this day, they have preserved their own ancient languages and dialects.

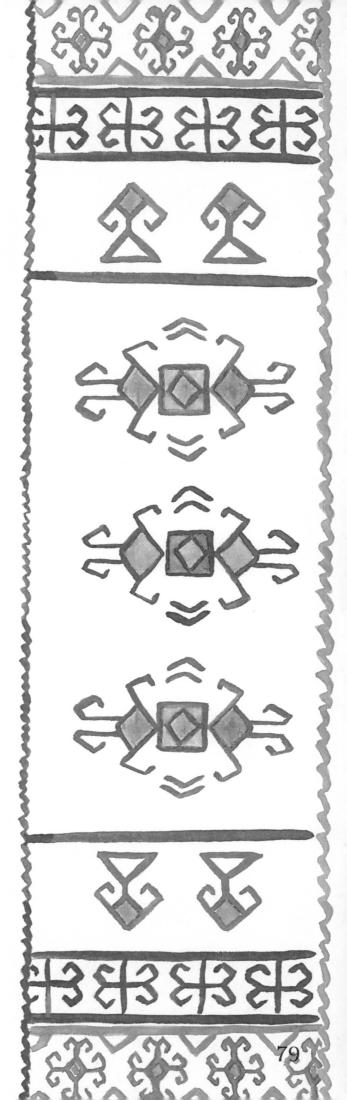

79

That is why many of the terms are wholly unique to certain regions of the country and many are specific just to a single community. Most of the terms seem to come from words meaning "feather," "to beat," "to pound," "to poke," or from "stick," "sign," or "symbol."

Here is the list of words for nonpar that I gathered from Tajikistan:

Nonpár	Parák	Goolzán
Moohpár	Parkoob	Dookkí
Mehpár	Nonparzanák	Kilch
Noohpár	Parzanák	Pish
Goolpár	Holzanák	Chikísh
Poorchook	Holchoob	Chekích
Parkooták	Nonchoobák	

Bakers in Central Asia show considerable inventiveness not just in decorating their *non* but in marketing them. Some bakers will use a tool to imprint their name and phone number onto each loaf. This way customers and their guests can call the baker directly to order the *non* that they liked.

Apricots

Apricots! It is impossible to picture childhood in Central Asia without these succulent, orange-yellow fruits, whether plucked fresh and juicy, made into homemade jam, or dried into sweet, chewy snacks. From the slopes of high mountains to the valleys, or to people's courtyards and gardens, apricots everywhere, like thousands upon thousands of little suns, announce the beginning of summer.

This fruit is one of the most nutritious in the world, containing iron, iodine, potassium, magnesium, phosphorus, carotene, vitamins A, B1, B2, B5, B3, B6, C, E, P, and PP, ascorbic acid, sugar and sucrose, and antioxidants. Apricots promote growth in children, improve memory, raise hemoglobin levels in the blood, strengthen immunity, reduce fatigue, and even help alleviate inflammation.

No one knows for sure where apricots originally came from. Europeans thought they came from Armenia and, because of this, gave the fruit the Latin name *Prúnus armeniáca*. Later, evidence was found showing apricot cultivation in ancient China and India. We can be sure of one thing – humans have been harvesting apricots for at least five thousand years!

Thanks to all of those vitamins and minerals, people have also used apricots as medicine. For example, doctors in ancient China mixed the fruit pulp with wax as a dressing for wounds. In ancient Egypt, crushed apricot pits were used as a remedy for laryngitis. Even the leaves, bark, and roots of the apricot tree were used for medical purposes (and still are!).

The pharaoh's subjects created many lotions and cosmetics from apricots, such as scrubs and apricot milk. Nowadays, doctors may prescribe dried apricots suffering from heart disease as they are high in potassium, which is good for the heart.

It is not surprising to find hundreds of recipes for cooking with this magic fruit from across the globe. People in the Pamirs even cook a soup made from dried apricots called *noshhoohpá* and another soup, *homni-gool*, made from ground apricot seeds, which they say fights colds and strengthens immunity.

The ancient masters created beautiful things with apricot wood such as exquisite furniture, musical wind instruments, and folding hand fans. The Egyptians made beads, bracelets, and earrings out of carved apricot pits. And spectacular Chinese craftsmen managed to carve figurines out of apricot pits so fine, that many of their details can only be seen under a magnifying glass!

Do you remember how Barzu's grandmother said that there were more than 300 varieties of apricots? As with *non*, apricots loom large in the culture and diet of Central Asia. In the Turkic languages of the region, this fruit is called *oruk, urik, örik,* or *erik,* while Tajik uses the word *zard-olú*. People sometimes use the Russian word *abrikós* to refer to a larger, juicier type of apricot.

Best of all are ripe apricots, fresh off the tree, but summer ends quickly and drying the fruit beneath the sun is the best way to preserve most of the vitamins and minerals for the rest of the year. In English we just call these dried apricots, while Russian uses the word *kooragá*, adapted from the Uzbek *kooroogí*, meaning "something dried." In Central Asia itself, however, *kooragá* only refers to more commercially-prepared dried apricots, that are larger with a brighter, yellow-orange color that is more appealing for the marketplace. Naturally-dried apricots, such as the ones drying on roofs in the story, have a darker and browner hue. Local people prefer the less attractive but more natural product, of which there are dozens of varieties, all with different names.

There are common names for apricots dried with the pit still intact: *goolíng, hooshkák, chamboor, toorshák, goloom, keshté, kok, kak,* and *kepkén*. Whole dried fruit without the pit is called *kaisá, bargák (bargék), sykmá* or *dolák*. Dried apricots that have the pit removed and are then split open to dry, without separating the two halves, is called *hashták*, from the Persian word for "eight," *hasht*, which is what the apricot now resembles.

The dried apricots are also classified according to their variety. For example, *kandák* (or *kandék*) is the sweetest dried apricot in the region. Other kinds are called *mokhtobí, soobkhoní, hooshk, goolkák, koormaí, isfarák,* and *kasiyék*.

There are also the marvelous varieties *mavizák* (or *koorooták*) and *mirsanjali*, which do not fall from the tree when ripe but dry out

directly on the branch! At the end of summer, people shake the trunk of the trees and collect the fallen, dried fruit from the ground.

Since dried apricots can be quite hard, people often soak them in water for a few hours. The apricots will soften, expand, and infuse the water with sweet, thick apricot nectar. This kind of drink is called *goolingób*.

Caravans

A *caravan* is a group of people and pack animals transporting loads of goods across the steppes and deserts. The types of pack animals used would vary depending on where the caravan came from and the length and geography of the route: from donkeys and mules to horses, camels, or even elephants. The convoy was led by the *Caravan-Bashi*, or Caravan Head, who knew the route best, followed by the animal drivers and armed guards. Merchants, scholars, pilgrims, and anyone else who needed to get from one point to another could also join the caravan.

Do you remember how the merchant Faiz traveled with his caravan to far-off Hindustan? What kind of animals appeared in those illustrations? The original sketches for those drawings included a donkey, dogs, and women travelers. However, given the length of the merchant's journey, I decided to consult with historian Stanislav A. Potapov on what the caravan would actually look like. Dr. Potapov was once my history teacher and is now a Research Fellow at the A. Kh. Margulan Institute of Archeology of the Academy of the Republic of Kazakhstan, as well as the Director of the Club for Historical Reconstruction and Historical Fencing. He has given permission to quote his correspondence with me:

In a typical caravan of an average, not poor, merchant, there were camels and guard horses. The horses were always kept away from the camels. Camels do not like horses and often attack them. The horses in a caravan would only carry armed guards, with the guards switching out up to three horses a day, to give each one time to rest.

Sometimes, rarely, among poorer caravans, there could be donkeys or mules. Poorer caravans did not have guards and engaged in smaller and less prosperous trade at a more local level. Caravans had to carry a lot of cargo not connected with trade: water, food, feed for the animals, tents. A donkey may carry no more than 15-20 kilograms (33-44 pounds) of merchandise, while a camel could take up to 70 kilograms (154 pounds). And the camel could walk faster and for longer without rest or water despite walking under these heavy loads. Dogs were not used. A caravan could cover 40 to 70 kilometers (24 to 43 miles) a day.

There could be women in a caravan. They would, often, join to travel from one point to another. But these women were not, so to speak, employees of the caravan. They did no work, except for specific instances, such as caring for someone's child or escorting a bride to her groom.

The caravan travelers did not have an easy time – they moved under the scorching sun, wind, and cold, and were under constant threat of marauding bandits. They tried to move as quickly as possible to the nearest *caravansarai* (or *caravansary*) – inns where the entourage could rest, eat, and drink. The *caravansarai* (from Persian *karwan* – "caravan," *sarai* – "palace") was a rectangular, fortified building with an inner courtyard, in the center of which was a well. The largest caravansarais could include a *chaikhana* (teahouse) with evening musical performances, a bath, a mosque, and a hospital. There travelers could also exchange money and news, or obtain a loan. Often, entire cities would grow up around the *caravansarai*.

Hindustan

Hindustan is an archaic (old and no longer used) word for the Indian subcontinent, what is now mostly India and Pakistan. Historically, the name comes from the Persian word meaning "the land of the Hindus" – the people who inhabited the Indus Valley. Persians, and then Europeans, most often thought of Hindustan as the territory between the Indus and Ganges rivers in the north and the Vindhya mountains in the south.

The Mughal Empire

Central Asia played an important role in the history and culture of the Indian subcontinent. In 1483, in the city of Andijan (now a part of Uzbekistan), Zahir ad-Din Mohammed Babur was born – the founder of the great Mughal empire, which occupied the territories of modern India, Pakistan, Bangladesh and southeastern Afghanistan.

Born into the family of Umar-Sheikh-Mirza II, Emir (king) of Ferghana and the great-grandson of Tamerlane, Babur fought for the Samarkand crown and dreamed of rebuilding the Timurid Empire. But Babur's rival, Sheibani Khan, the leader of the nomadic Uzbek tribes, was stronger and forced Babur out into the territory of present-day Afghanistan. This setback did not break Babur: first, he became the ruler of Kabul, and by 1529 he conquered north-west Hindustan. Over time, his descendants expanded the boundaries of the empire, moving further south.

All members of the Babur dynasty proudly called themselves Timurids, after their ancestor Tamerlane. Where did the word "Mughals" come from?

The word is the Persian pronunciation for "Mongol," because Babur and his army came from the lands of the old Mongol empire. Rulers in the region still traced their ancestry back to the great Genghis Khan and Babur's mother was considered a direct descendant of the Mongol conqueror.

Bibi-Khanym Mosque
(1404, Samarkand, Uzbekistan)

Gur-i Amir (family tomb of Tamerlane,
1404, Samarkand, Uzbekistan)

Tomb of Humayun (1570, Delhi, India)

Mausoleum of Akbar (1613, Sikandra, India)

Mausoleum of Jahangir
(1637, Lahore, Pakistan)

Mausoleum of Itmad-Ud-Dawla (1628, Agra, India)

Taj Mahal (1653, Agra, India)

The Mughal dynasty lasted for over 300 years, from 1526 to 1858. Many books have been written about Babur himself – and not just as a conqueror but also as a poet, gardener, historian, geographer, and ethnographer – and about each of his descendants. But what is important for us is how Babur's arrival spread Islamic religion and Persian culture so widely through the Indian subcontinent. This merged with the local traditions to create a unique civilization, an amazing blend of Islamic, Hindu, Buddhist and Christian styles. Today, Mughal architectural marvels in Agra, Fatehpur-Sikri, Lahore, Delhi and other cities attract millions of tourists annually from all over the world.

The famous Taj Mahal, the mausoleum erected by Shah Jahan from 1631 to 1653 in honor of his beloved wife, is considered the architectural peak of Mughal style. Here we can see the strong influence of Samarkand, particularly Bibi-Khanym Mosque and Gur-i Amir (Gur-Emir), both of which Shah Jahan carefully studied.

Another example is the tomb of Humayun, Babur's son, built in Delhi from 1562 to 1570. It was designed by an architect who had practiced in Bukhara for many years. The plan of four symmetrical towers surrounding a massive portal comes directly from Bukhara and had a great impact on future Mughal buildings. We also see a strong Timurid influence in the mausoleums of Akbar (1613, Sikandra, India), Itmad-Ud-Dawla (1628, Agra, India) and Jahangir (1637, Lahore, Pakistan), each surrounded by four minarets with rich interior decoration reminiscent of Tamerlane's capital.

The City of the Sun

The city of Jodhpur is known as Sun City for the clear, sunny weather it enjoys in summer and winter, in the state of Rajasthan, on the outskirts of the Tar desert in India. This is the homeland of the proud Rajputs – an age-old people whose ethnic origin scholars have not yet established. For Rajputs, freedom and independence have always been more valuable than life, and few succeeded in completely subjugating them. Even when they were part of the Mughal empire, and later the British colony, they still retained their autonomy.

Back in 1459, the Rajput ruler Rao Jodha founded Jodhpur, which became the capital of his state, then called Marwar ("Land of Death" in Sanskrit, in reference to the lifeless, encircling deserts). In the same year, at the top of the hill towering over the city, he began construction of Mehrangarh, the Fortress of the Sun (In Sanskrit *mehir* means "sun" and *garh* means "fortress") which stands to this day, resembling a mighty giant glaring out menacingly over the desert expanses. Rao Jodha's successors added to Mehrangarh over the next 500 years. Behind its tall, red walls of 21 meters (68 feet) in thickness and seven gates hide gardens, squares, courtyards, and several palaces with fabulous names, such as the Palace of Pearls or the Palace of Glimpses.

What makes the fortress unique is how it blends its military function with a pleasing aesthetic style. The fortress is a perfect example of medieval defensive architecture, designed to protect and repel, while its inner buildings show that the Rajput princes were great connoisseurs of the arts. Its elegant stone carvings, sophisticated wall decorations, whimsical floral motifs, openwork arches of balconies and windows delight visitors. Stone laces change color during the day from almost white to dark red, creating a sense of magic.

Holidays in Rajasthan are always filled with a variety of festive clothes, and the rhythms and melodies of local instruments. The illustrations to the chapter *The Bread of Wonder* introduce readers to three popular dances in Jodhpur – *dandiya gher (gair)*, *kachi ghodi* and *bhavai*.

In the *dandiya gher*, men and women move in a circle in opposite directions, tapping wooden sticks in the rhythm of the drums. Rhythmic sounds and rotating movements create a hypnotic spectacle. Men are usually dressed in long, flared tunics and turbans. The wooden *dandiya* sticks that are used in this dance symbolize the sword of the warrior goddess Durga – defender of the gods and the world order, fighter of demons. According to Hinduism, one of the most ancient religions of the world, there are more than 3,000 gods, goddesses, and divine animals.

The dance of *kachi ghodi* is like a comic performance. A troupe of actors and musicians, through funny songs and dances, tells the viewer about the unfortunate adventures of the merchants traveling in their caravans. Actors on ragged horses depict them fending off attacking bandits.

Bhavai is performed by women. The dancer, in a colorful dress, balances up to a dozen pitchers on her head, while dancing to music with complex foot movements. *Bhavai* has its roots in those times when women went with jars for water, often over long, hard distances.

Names

Barzú – This is a Persian name meaning "sublime" or "exalted." The hero Barzu holds a special place in Persian mythology and is the central character in an ancient, epic poem called *The Barzunoma*. The tale of Barzu follows a tragic story, in which the father Rustam accidentally kills his son Sukhrob in battle. Sukhrob's son, Barzu, grows up without a father and his mother raises him alone. As fate would have it, he is one day captured by his own grandfather, who does not know him. Barzu's mother reaches Rustam in time to tell him who his hostage is, saving her son from execution.

These legends have been passed on from generation to generation, told at gatherings on winter evenings, especially in far-off kishlaks. Residents of the highlands of Boysun in Uzbekistan believe that Barzu was born there. And in the Rushan region of Tajikistan's Pamir mountains, there are the two kishlaks of Barzud and Derzud, named in honor of Barzu and his brother Derzu, who they believe are the protectors of their villages.

Zafár – "Victory," Arabic.

Ravshán – "Bright soul," Persian.

Sitóra – "Star," Persian.

Lóla – "Tulip," or "Spring Flower," Persian.

Faíz – "Generous" in Persian, also "Winner" in Arabic.

Sardár – "Commander" or "General," Persian.

Azhdár – "Dragon," Persian. Also pronounced "Azhdahór."

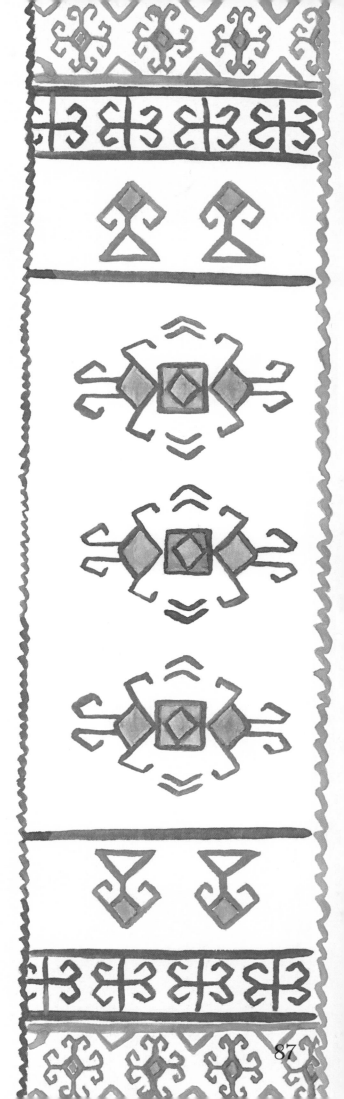

Ethnography

Ethnography is the study of people and cultures, their customs, traditions, and history. Ethnographers observe the defining features of a society, including their language, family and social relationships, self-perception, and historical associations.

Kizyak (Dung Fuel)

In the days before electricity or gas, people would use whatever natural materials were available for heating or cooking. And it turned out that dried animal manure burns very well, particularly that of cattle, sheep, or horses. This was absolutely free fuel!

It is still used, even now, in many parts of the world. Throughout the summer people will collect animal manure, sometimes mix it with straw, form it into round cakes or square bricks and dry them under the sun. You can find neatly stacked piles of these bricks in nearly every courtyard of every home in the villages of Central Asia (and, by the way, you can also see them in the illustrations for "The Secrets of Master Zafar").

English does not have a particular name for dried dung fuel but in Russian (my first language), we call it *kizyák*, while the people of Central Asia use different names, such as *tizyák, tezék, tappí, tapák, jampá, koomalák,* or *hoomalák.*

Nomads vs Settled People

Nomads are people who move from one place to another. This way of life is found mostly in places where the climate makes settled agriculture impossible, such as on the steppe (arid grasslands), in deserts, or mountains. Nomads are primarily livestock breeders and are always moving around in search of good pasture. Nomads are also excellent hunters.

Over the course of human evolution, many people learned to cultivate land and grow food. They stopped moving in search of food, built their own homes and began to live in one place. That is, they began to lead a sedentary lifestyle.

The Silk Road

The Silk Road stretched for about 7,000 kilometers (about 23,000 miles). Merchants used this road to bring products such as tea, rice, silk, china, bronze products, medicines, perfumes, umbrellas, carpets, and wool from Asia to Europe.

India was an important source of spices (saffron, pepper, ginger, turmeric and others), gems, ivory, dyes, fabrics, and incense.

The Chinese imported majestic horses, camels, carpets, glassware, and military equipment from Central Asia. The Chinese particularly appreciated the exotic – for them – fruits and vegetables of Central Asia, such as grapes, watermelons, melons, peaches, pomegranate, figs, carrots, cucumbers, beans, and onions.

The Pamirs

Snow-covered mountains and valleys form the vast Pamir Highland (Pamir) in the south of Central Asia, stretching across Afghanistan, China, Kyrgyzstan, Pakistan, and Tajikistan. The Pamirs are amongst the highest mountains in the world. Mount Kongur in China is 7,649 meters (over 25,000 feet) above sea level, and the peak of Mount Ismail Somoni in Tajikistan reaches 7,495 meters (24,589 feet). It's no wonder the Pamirs are called, like the Himalayas, the "Roof of the World."

About 12 different ethnic and linguistic groups live in the Pamirs and each group is made up of between 100 and 110,000 people. Where they all came from, living at such altitudes, cut off from the rest of civilization, is a mystery. Some historians believe they came to the mountains to escape persecution or attack by invaders.

Living in settlements isolated from each other with only limited access by the narrowest roads helped each group preserve its own unique language. It is interesting to note that the Pamir languages (apart from the Turkic language of the Pamir Kyrgyz) are part of a different subgroup of Iranian languages than Tajik, which means Tajiks and Pamiris have a hard time understanding each other.

The climate in the Pamir is very harsh with long winters. The architecture of houses, food, and clothing here is very different, as the life and culture of the people are fully geared to survival in a difficult environment.

The Pamiri people love their homeland for its unique nature and beauty.

Union of Soviet Socialist Republics (USSR)

The USSR, or the Soviet Union, existed from 1922 to 1991 and, at the time of its collapse, was the largest country in the world. Its capital was in Moscow. The Soviet Union included the following republics, which subsequently became independent states (using their current names):

Azerbaijan, Armenia, Belarus, Georgia, Estonia, Kazakhstan, Kyrgyzstan, Latvia, Lithuania, Moldova, Russia, Tajikistan, Turkmenistan, Uzbekistan, and Ukraine.

Chaikhana

The literal translation of *chaikhana* is "teahouse." This was the traditional gathering place for men to discuss business, share the latest news, or listen to the stories of some traveling merchant. Proprietors would build their teahouses in the shade of trees or near a pond, so that visitors could relax on *topchans* on hot days. Large *caravansarais* offered travelers the services of a teahouse, where, in addition to tea, food was also served.

Chaikhanas continue to exist to this day, although in large cities they have become more like a modern cafe.

About the Authors

Marina Abrams is the founder of Barzu World, which promotes awareness about the countries of Central Asia through publications, art projects, and events. Marina graduated from the Translation-Interpretation Department at the Abylaikhan Kazakh State University of International Relations and World Languages in Almaty, Kazakhstan. In addition to English, she studied Chinese and Spanish. Marina received her M.A. in International Policy Studies at Monterey Institute of International Studies (now the Middlebury Institute of International Studies at Monterey) in California. She lives in Maryland, USA, with her husband and two beautiful children. This is the first in Marina's *World of Barzu* book series.

Farrukh Negmatzade is a well-known, contemporary artist of Tajikistan. Farrukh studied at the prestigious Moscow Art School under the Academy of Arts of the USSR and the Moscow Surikov State Art Institute. His works are exhibited in galleries and private collections around the world. He lives with his family in Dushanbe, Tajikistan.

Sponsors of the book

 Tajik American Cultural Association

 The Central Asia Program, George Washington University

 Tajik Bakery in Virginia, USA

 Center for Languages of the Central Asian Region, Indiana University

James Martin
Howard Fishman
Vita Abrams
Sol Abrams

Abid Hussain
Adila Musayeva
Agata Ianturina
Aidyn Bibolov
Aigerim Arynova-Berger
Aika Crumrine
Ainash YP
Ainur Simon
Ainura Absemetova
Ainura Tursunova
Akaki Dvali
Akmaral Alimzhan
Albina Torosyan
Alena Fielding
Alexander Starostin
Alice O'Donovan
Alijon Sharipov
Alma Jaxybayeva
Alvilda Jablonko
Amanda Sharp

Amber Kennedy Kent
Amber Rexilius
Ambrose Dieringer
Andy Offenbacher
Anita Kolaczkowska
Anna Agranovich
Anna Belousova
Anna Borovikov
Anna Cohen Miller
Anna Smeby
Anna Svizhenko
Anna Weis
Antoine Buisson
Ari Katz
Arman Kassengali
Artem Goncharuk
Arthur Van Diesen
Arzygul Madalimova
Avgerinos Markopoulos
Axelle Nos
Aziz
Bahromjon Rabiev
Beth Sheehy
Beverly Wang
Bintou Camara

Brenda and Don Grauer
Brian Varrieur
Carol and Dennis Friedman
Catherine Gabb
Catherine Range
Chris Jensen
Christina Maple Ferguson
Christina Watts
Christine Tefft
Christopher Miller
Chuck Rice
Courtney Zenz
Cynthia Buckley
Dagmar
Damira Khatam
Dana Tumenova
Danara Dukembayeva
Daria Kirichenko
Daria Sinitsyna
Darya Bukhtoyarova
David Blood
Davide and Alessia Costa
Deborah Sher
Denise Ifkovic
Destouches Benoit

Diana Nezamutinova

Diane Mones

Dilafruz Nazarova

Dilnoza Azamova

Dina Adilbekova

Dina Schneider

Dinara Turegeldiyeva

Dinissa Duvanova

Dmitri Matveev

DobrajaKsu

Eileen McVey

Ekaterina Skliarova

Elaine Abrams

Elena Bennett

Elena Cirmizi

Elena Klintsova

Elena Kornilova

Elena Scheslavskaya

Elena Stungis

Elena Voronova

Elina Lyu

Elina Troscenko

Elise-Sophie Kuimcheva

Elizabeth Cameron

Elizabeth Chambers

Elizabeth Horst

Elizabeth Turnock

Elmira Freeman

Elvira Metoff

Emma Sabzalieva

Emmanuel Huntzinger

Eric Ronning

Erik Pugner

Estelle Dauchy

Evan Dawley

Evgeniya Gomon

Evgeniya Usmanova

Faruhbek

Feruza Abdullaeva

Firuza Shamsieva

Firuza Umarova

Frances and Keith Huckle

Gabriela Saakova

Gascoin Olivier

Gaukhar Mukhatzhanova

Geni Achnas

Guest 181313785

Gulnar Nagashybayeva

Gulnoza Tulyaganova

Guly Sabahi

Guvanch Meredov

Hannah Anderson

Heather Worley Torrance

Helen Nordloh

Ingrida Diurbeiko

Inna Moon

Irina Glabuchek

Irina Prudovskaya

Irina Zhygalko

Iskandar Rafiev

Iuliia Larina

Ivana Sirovic

Ivetta Starikova

Jahongir Usmanov

James and Karina Ayres

Jamie De Luce

Jane Kurbat

Jason and Sharon Franklin

Jeffrey Whitbeck

Jeni Washeleski

Jes and Mad Dennett

Jessica Hayden

Jill Davies

Jodi Rafkin

Judith Skartvedt

Julia Dautov

Kaitlyn Bartley

Karen Lewis

Katerena Alkhimova

Katherine Gordy

Katherine Magalif

Kathy Shats

Katya Shterenberg

Keith Mellnick

Kennedy Schultz

Keya Bayramova

Khushnuda Shukurova

Kimberley Fortin

Kimberly Zenz

Kirill Kuzmin

Kirsten Oleson

Kitty Purgason

Ksenia Eremeeva

Ksenia Turkova

Kuowei Eleazar Chiu

Kuralay Sarkitova

Laina Reynolds Levy

Laura Tourtellotte

Lauren Maze

Laurie Tyre

Laylee Moshiri

Leila Emerson

Lena Kirochko-Murray

Leo A. Gulamov

Lilia Karimova

Linketto

Lisa Neel

Lola Lunstrum

Lola Luton

Louis Gigout

Lufench

Luz Campoli

Maddy

Madina Toshmuhamedova

Madina Yusupova

Mae Esperon-Jabrayilova

Manana and Rob O'Donovan

Marc Liberati

Marcela and Pablo Campoli

Marco Rossi

Margarita Sevcik

Margarita Yukhno

Mari Paajanen

Maria Abramovitch

Maria Adamian

Maria Blackwood

Maria Carmona

Maria Ivanteeva

Maria Jahromi

Maria Rausse

Maria Tcherni

Marianne Kamp

Marina Carter

Marina Chernova

Marina Ivanovskaya

Marina Kalinin

Marina Malinov

Marina Matveeva-Melnik

Mark and Olga Hannafin

Mark Cullen

Mark Furstenberg

Mark Hurley

Mark Tang

Mark Veevers-Carter

Martin and Emily Daughtry

Mary Beth and Alexander Nikitin

Masha Saunders

Masha Sumaroka Nikolayev

Matlyuba Karimi

Matthew Mulherin

Maureen Bartee

Maureen Taft-Morales

Maya Saryeva

Mayya Lavrenko

mbakanova

Mehrangez Rafieva

Mehri Kar

Merchimerch

Meredith Sopher

Merey Ismailova

Michael and Adelya Downward

Michael and Liz

Michael Andrews Bashan

Michael Boud

Michael Hickey

Michael O'Brien

Michael Smolyak

Michelle Reichert

Mikhail Romanyuk

Mila Bebe

Milan and Matisse Nichilo

Mina Madani

Mitchell Wiener

Mollie Pugh

Morgane La Fée

Mubinjon Satymov

Muborak Sharipova

Nadiya Mastri

Nadya Nikiforova

Nafisa Khussenova

Namrita Singh

Nasiba Sharipova

Natalia Novitskaya

Natalia Pcholkina

Natalia Saraeva

Natalia Susak

Nataliia Toropova

Natalya and Andrew Grauer

Natascha Bohlmann

Natasha and Michail Mirny

Natasha Bajema

Natasha Pfleger

Nazira Abdukhalilova

Nelli Baltabayeva

Nicole Davis

Nicole Esquenet

Nicolo Viegener

Nigina Normatova

Nigina Valentini

Nisso and Dan Stanley

Nodir Zakirov

Noila and Wade Sorenson

Nona Langley

Nuket Kardam

Nuria Gabitova

Odalis F. Marte

Oigul Karimova-Cadé

Oksana Falbo

Olesya Menon

Olga and Mila Dzharimbetova

Olga Eromenko

Olga Knorre

Olga Meleshko

Olga Rakhmatullova

Olwyn Flett

Olya Reghay

Oscar and Maddy McCardle

Oxana Ritz

Patricia Sosa

Patricia Veevers-Carter

Pavel Sinev

Pilar Lenora Robledo

Polina Voinevych

Raisa Glushko

Raquel Rodriguez

Rauf Abduzhalilov

Renata Holmen

Rene Lindenthal

Rich Bailey

Robin Lee Reed

Roe Alan

Romany Redman

Roxana Gabdul

Rubi Vasquez

Rustam Koralbasayev

Rusty "The Sandman"
Shackleford

Safarsho Merob

Sandy Barry Gally

Sarah Jane Dixon Klump

Saule Kassengaliyeva

Sean and Kristen Crocker

Shahnoz Eronshoh

Shahnoza Moore

Shahnoza Muminzoda

Shahnozakhon Muminzoda

Shakhlo Sharipova

Shakhnoza Bakhodyrovna

Shakhnoza Yunusova

Shauna Barr

Shavkat Shamukhamedov

Shoira Yusupova

Sonia Ben Ouagrham-Gormley

Speed Franklin

Stanley Currier

Stephanie Riis-Due Zayouna

Steven Perry

Sue Parkes

Suiunay Amanalieva

Summer Coish

Susan Helms Daley

Susan M Elliott

Suzanne Boutilier

Svetlana Reznikov

Svetlana Velkovsky

Symbat Zhumanova

Tahmina Hakimova-Rees

Takhmina Namozova

Tamara Kalandia

Tania Pushcashu

Tatiana Benner

Tatiana Platova

Tatiana Vinogradova

Tatiana Whatley

The Creative Fund

The Raitt family

Theresa Cauble

Timothy Walsh

Timur Pusimennii

Togzhan Kassenova

Tokhir Mirzoev

Tom Hickerson

Troy Etulain

Ulyana Panchishin

Ulyana Willoughby

Umed Babakhanov

Utkirdjan Umarov

Valeri and Lyubov Baratov

Valerie Moinard-Negaret

Vera Markovich

Vera Zolotarskaya

Veronique Geoffroy

Victoria Charbonneau

Victoria Gabrielyan

Victoria Kuimcheva

Viony Medlin

Vladislav Fedorov

Vostok

William A Barnes

William Veale

Xi Yin

Yana Dimitrovich

Yana Khater

Yana Paton

Yana Zabanova

Yelena Nichilo

Yev Yegorov

Yevgeny Liokumovich

Yoanna Gouchtchina

Yolonda Richardson

Yulenka Kulyk

Yulia Drobova

Zarrina Akhmedova

Zarrina Babakulova

Zarrina Juraqulova

Zarrina Sarbarova

Zere Kabyl-Fazyl

Zulfira Pulotova

Contents

BARZU WORLD

Orange and Blue: The World of Barzu

Second edition 2018

ISBN: 978-1-5323-8911-5

Printed in *From A to Z* (Kyiv, Ukraine)

Technical and logistical support by publishing house *Yarnika* (Kyiv, Ukraine)

Editing by Natalia Kuzmina and by Joanne with Firstediting.com

Computer design by Natalia Didenko, Alex Mintz, Eugenia Makarova, Yulia Lukashova

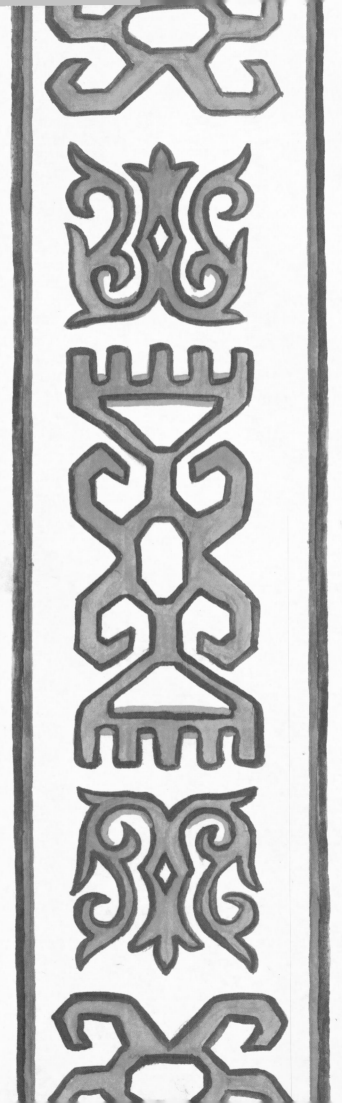